FRANCIS FRITH'S

HAMPSHIRE

LIVING MEMORIES

TIMOTHY ALLETSON SAUNDERS is the advertisement manager for 'HAMPSHIRE *the county magazine*' - the oldest independent magazine in Hampshire and the only one authorised to carry the prestigious county crest on its cover. Tim is also a freelance journalist contributing to newspapers and magazines. Educated at Dorchester Preparatory School and Clayesmore School, he took A-levels at Weymouth College and read a business and law degree at Southampton Institute. Tim is 26 years old and a keen historian. For more information visit http://www.geocities.com/c8tas

FRANCIS FRITH'S
PHOTOGRAPHIC MEMORIES

HAMPSHIRE
LIVING MEMORIES

TIMOTHY ALLETSON SAUNDERS

First published in the United Kingdom in 2005 by
Frith Book Company Ltd

Hardback Edition 2005
ISBN 1-85937-527-8

British Library Cataloguing in Publication Data

Francis Frith's Hampshire Living Memories
Timothy Alletson Saunders

Frith Book Company Ltd
Frith's Barn, Teffont,
Salisbury, Wiltshire SP3 5QP
Tel: +44 (0) 1722 716 376
Email: info@francisfrith.co.uk
www.francisfrith.co.uk

Printed and bound in Great Britain

Front Cover: **NETHER WALLOP,** *The Square c1955* N156001t
Frontispiece: **ALTON,** *Crown Hill c1955* A39097

*The colour-tinting is for illustrative purposes only, and is not intended to be
historically accurate*

AS WITH ANY HISTORICAL DATABASE THE FRITH ARCHIVE IS CONSTANTLY
BEING CORRECTED AND IMPROVED, AND THE PUBLISHERS WOULD
WELCOME INFORMATION ON OMISSIONS OR INACCURACIES

Acknowledgements
With many thanks to Caroline for her help, support and
advice, and to my family for their useful input.

CONTENTS

FRANCIS FRITH
VICTORIAN PIONEER

FRANCIS FRITH, founder of the world-famous photographic archive, was a complex and multi-talented man. A devout Quaker and a highly successful Victorian businessman, he was philosophical by nature and pioneering in outlook.

By 1855 he had already established a wholesale grocery business in Liverpool, and sold it for the astonishing sum of £200,000, which is the equivalent today of over £15,000,000. Now a very rich man, he was able to indulge his passion for travel. As a child he had pored over travel books written by early explorers, and his fancy and imagination had been stirred by family holidays to the sublime mountain regions of Wales and Scotland. 'What lands of spirit-stirring and enriching scenes and places!' he had written. He was to return to these scenes of grandeur in later years to 'recapture the thousands of vivid and tender memories', but with a different purpose. Now in his thirties, and captivated by the new science of photography, Frith set out on a series of pioneering journeys up the Nile and to the Near East that occupied him from 1856 until 1860.

INTRIGUE AND EXPLORATION

These far-flung journeys were packed with intrigue and adventure. In his life story, written when he was sixty-three, Frith tells of being held captive by bandits, and of fighting 'an awful midnight battle to the very point of surrender with a deadly pack of hungry, wild dogs'. Wearing flowing Arab costume, Frith arrived at Akaba by camel sixty years before Lawrence of Arabia, where he encountered 'desert princes and rival sheikhs, blazing with jewel-hilted swords'.

He was the first photographer to venture beyond the sixth cataract of the Nile. Africa was still the mysterious 'Dark Continent', and Stanley and Livingstone's historic meeting was a decade into the future. The conditions for picture taking confound belief. He laboured for hours in his wicker dark-room in the sweltering heat of the desert, while the volatile chemicals fizzed dangerously in their trays. Back in London he exhibited his photographs and was 'rapturously cheered' by members of the Royal Society. His reputation as a photographer was made overnight.

VENTURE OF A LIFE-TIME

Characteristically, Frith quickly spotted the opportunity to create a new business as a specialist publisher of photographs. He lived in an era of immense and sometimes violent change. For the poor in the early part of Victoria's reign work was exhausting and the hours long, and people had precious little free time to enjoy themselves. Most people had no transport other than a cart or gig at their disposal, and rarely

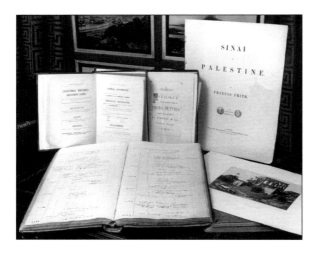

business one only has to look at the catalogue issued by Frith & Co in 1886: it runs to some 670 pages, listing not only many thousands of views of the British Isles but also many photographs of most European countries, and China, Japan, the USA and Canada - note the sample page shown on page 9 from the hand-written Frith & Co ledgers recording the pictures. By 1890 Frith had created the greatest specialist photographic publishing company in the world, with over 2,000 sales outlets - more than the combined number that Boots and WH Smith have today! The picture on the nest page shows the Frith & Co display board at Ingleton in the Yorkshire Dales (left of window). Beautifully constructed with a mahogany frame and gilt inserts, it could display up to a dozen local scenes.

POSTCARD BONANZA

The ever-popular holiday postcard we know today took many years to develop. In 1870 the Post Office issued the first plain cards, with a pre-printed stamp on one face. In 1894 they allowed other publishers' cards to be sent through the mail with an attached adhesive halfpenny stamp. Demand grew rapidly, and in 1895 a new size of postcard was permitted called the court card, but there was little room for illustration. In 1899, a year after Frith's death, a new card measuring 5.5 x 3.5 inches became the standard format, but it was not until 1902 that the divided back came into being, so that the address and message could be on one face and a full-size illustration on the other. Frith & Co were in the vanguard of postcard development: Frith's sons Eustace and Cyril continued their father's monumental task, expanding the number of views offered to the public and recording more and more places in Britain, as the coasts and countryside were opened up to mass travel.

Francis Frith had died in 1898 at his villa in Cannes, his great project still growing. The archive he created continued in business for another seventy years. By 1970 it contained over a third of a million pictures showing 7,000 British towns and villages.

travelled far beyond the boundaries of their own town or village. However, by the 1870s the railways had threaded their way across the country, and Bank Holidays and half-day Saturdays had been made obligatory by Act of Parliament. All of a sudden the working man and his family were able to enjoy days out and see a little more of the world.

With typical business acumen, Francis Frith foresaw that these new tourists would enjoy having souvenirs to commemorate their days out. In 1860 he married Mary Ann Rosling and set out on a new career: his aim was to photograph every city, town and village in Britain. For the next thirty years he travelled the country by train and by pony and trap, producing fine photographs of seaside resorts and beauty spots that were keenly bought by millions of Victorians. These prints were painstakingly pasted into family albums and pored over during the dark nights of winter, rekindling precious memories of summer excursions.

THE RISE OF FRITH & CO

Frith's studio was soon supplying retail shops all over the country. To meet the demand he gathered about him a small team of photographers, and published the work of independent artist-photographers of the calibre of Roger Fenton and Francis Bedford. In order to gain some understanding of the scale of Frith's

St Catherine's College
Senate House & Library
Gerrard Hostel Bridge
Geological Museum
Addenbrooke's Hospital
St Mary's Church
Fitzwilliam Museum, Pitt Press &c
Buxton, The Crescent
   The Colonnade
   Public Gardens
Haddon Hall, View from the Terrace
Miller's Dale
Bakewell, Bridge &c
   Footbridge
   Church
   "   Interior
Matlock Bath, The High Tor
   " On the Derwent
   " Brunswood Terrace
   " Cliff &c

FRANCIS FRITH'S LEGACY

Frith's legacy to us today is of immense significance and value, for the magnificent archive of evocative photographs he created provides a unique record of change in the cities, towns and villages throughout Britain over a century and more. Frith and his fellow studio photographers revisited locations many times down the years to update their views, compiling for us an enthralling and colourful pageant of British life and character.

We are fortunate that Frith was dedicated to recording the minutiae of everyday life. For it is this sheer wealth of visual data, the painstaking chronicle of changes in dress, transport, street layouts, buildings, housing, engineering and landscape that captivates us so much today. His remarkable images offer us a powerful link with the past and with the lives of our ancestors.

THE VALUE OF THE ARCHIVE TODAY

Computers have now made it possible for Frith's many thousands of images to be accessed almost instantly. Frith's images are increasingly used as visual resources, by social historians, by researchers into genealogy and ancestry, by architects and town planners, and by teachers involved in local history projects.

In addition, the archive offers every one of us an opportunity to examine the places where we and our families have lived and worked down the years. Highly successful in Frith's own era, the archive is now, a century and more on, entering a new phase of popularity. Historians consider the Francis Frith Collection to be of prime national importance. It is the only archive of its kind remaining in private ownership. Francis Frith's archive is now housed in an historic timber barn in the beautiful village of Teffont in Wiltshire. Its founder would not recognize the archive office as it is today. In place of the many thousands of dusty boxes containing glass plate negatives and an all-pervading odour of photographic chemicals, there are now ranks of computer screens. He would be amazed to watch his images travelling round the world at unimaginable speeds through internet lines.

The archive's future is both bright and exciting. Francis Frith, with his unshakeable belief in making photographs available to the greatest number of people, would undoubtedly approve of what is being done today with his lifetime's work. His photographs depicting our shared past are now bringing pleasure and enlightenment to millions around the world a century and more after his death.

WILT (From East Lavington)

From Wilton

SALISBURY

DORSETSHIRE

WILTS

Nether Wallop · Leckford

Longstock

STOCKBRIDGE

Crawley

Houghton Drayton

Little Somborn

Littleton

Lainson

Broughton

Ashley

Sparsholt

Bossington

King's Somborn

WINCH

West Tytherley

Eltan

Farley Chamberlayne

East Tytherley

French Moor

Mottisfont

Mitchelmersh

Brushfield

Slackstead

Com

East Dean

Lockerley

Hursley

Sherfield English

Timsbury

Otterbour

Sa

Amphiel

Rackburne

Nth. Charford

Sth. Charford

East Wellow

Embley

Ri.

ROMSEY

Badderley North

Breamore

Hale

Wood Gr.

Ranvills

Chilworth

North Stoneha

Burgate

Godshill

Bramshaw

Nutshalling

South Stoneham

FORDINGBRIDGE

Fritham

Brook

Codnam

Testwood

Shirley

Portsm

Harbridge

Ibsley

NEW

Minstead

Eling

Millbrook

arys

Itchen

Ellingham

Linwood

FOREST

Lyndhurst

SOUTHAMPTON

Dibden

Ashley

Burley Lo.

Hythe

Southam

RINGWOOD

Burley

Bistern Closes

Beaulieu Riv.

From Wimborne Minster

Kingston

Brockenhurst

Beaulieu

Fawle

Avon Water

Boldre

River Avon

Shirley

Avon

Batramsley

Buckleshard

Exbury

Ower

Lan

R. Stour

Sopley

Hinton

Pennington

Buddesley

Holdenhurst

LYMINGTON

Milton

Ashley

Efford

THE SOLEN

CHRISTCHURCH

Hordle

Milford

Hurst Cas.

Yarmouth

Thorley

Newtown

I

Christchurch Bay

Freshwater

Shalfleet

Car

Hengistbury Head

Poole Bay

The Needles

Easton

Calbourn

Freshwater Bay

Brook

Mottiston

Brixton

Candover Wield Medsted East W...

Northington West Worldham Kingsley

Abbotston Swarraton Godsfield Chawton Hartley Headley

...ty Martyrs Worthy Itchin Abbots Bighton Faringdon Maudit Bramshott To

...s Worthy Itchin Old Alresford Ropley Stoke Selborne

Easton Avington Stoke Bishops Rotherfield Newton Valence

Winnal Ovington NEW ALRESFORD Sutton East Empshot

Magdalen Hill Titchbourn Ropley Tisted Colemore Greatham

Chilcomb Cheriton West Priors Hawkley Liss

Hinton Ampner Bramdean Tisted Dean

Morestead Kilmeston Filmer Hill Steep

Twyford Beaworth Privett Sheet

Owlesbury Warnford Peak Froxfield R. Rother

Upham West Meon Westbury Langrish PETERSFIELD

...p. Stoke Exton East Meon MIDHURST

Durley Corhampton Meon Stoke Fairfield Buriton South Amb...

BISHOPS WALTHAM Droxford Chidden Clanfield

Soberton Chalton Idsworth

Botley Hambledon Catherington Blendworth

Swanwick Elm Wickham Finch Dean

Southwick West Leigh

Boarhunt Widley Purbrook Warblington

Hamble en le Rice FAREHAM PORTSDOWN Hill HAVANT Emsworth CHICHESTER

Titchfield Wymering Farlington Bedhampton To Arund.

Hook Porchester Portsmouth North Hayling

Crofton Harbour Hilsea Langston West Thorney

...dshot ...us. Rowner Portsea Kingston Harbour Pilsey I.

GOSPORT Canal Sth Havling Langstn Harbour

Alverstoke PORTSMOUTH Selsea Bill

...es East Cowes SPITHEAD

Whippingham Binstead

Wooton Ryde

Medina R. Haven Str. St Helens

NEWPORT OF Brading Foreland

Arreton Brading Hbr.

Blackwaters Yaverland

...comb ...ookley Newchurch

GHT

HAMPSHIRE
LIVING MEMORIES
AN INTRODUCTION

BEFORE the time of Elizabeth I, few people knew what their county looked like. In 1579 Andrew Saxton published his first map recognising individual counties and this marked the beginning of people's interest in local topography. Now, we all know something about the county we live in, even if this is just where it lies in relation to others. Great Britain is made up of 86 counties, and Hampshire is one of the most popular places to live and to visit. It is half way between the east and west ends of the south coast. To the west it is bordered by Dorset and Wiltshire; Berkshire is to the north; and to the east are Surrey and West Sussex. Hampshire's southern coastline is on the Solent, the strait separating the Isle of Wight from mainland Britain. Being only a couple of hours away from London, Hampshire is ideal commuter territory.

After Yorkshire, Hampshire is the next largest county in the United Kingdom, and offers something to everyone: it has countryside, beaches,

CADNAM, *The Sir John Barleycorn c1960* C3012

shopping centres, attractions, and plenty of history. It is home to the sprawling New Forest that covers 145 square miles. Still largely owned by the Crown, it is managed by the Forestry Enterprise (part of the Forestry Commission). The land that is not owned by the Crown is either privately owned or open forest. Now a national park, it is a nationally important environment of woodland pasture, heaths, bogs, coppices, and timber plantations. It is grazed by locally owned ponies, cattle and pigs. Here you will find both Exbury Gardens, owned by the well-known Rothschild family, and Beaulieu Motor Museum.

Hampshire includes three unique cities. That cannot be said of many counties. These are Winchester, Portsmouth, and Southampton. Hampshire's oldest city is Winchester, also Hampshire's county town, an unspoilt cathedral city on the edge of the South Downs. It is the ancient capital of England, the former seat and principal city of King Alfred the Great, who reigned between 871 and 899. The Norman-built Winchester Cathedral took 14 years to erect, and was completed in 1093. One of the longest cathedrals in Europe, it measures 556ft in length. Jane Austen is buried here. Winchester is home to Winchester College, founded by William of Wykeham, who was the great bishop of Winchester in 1382. Many hundreds of years later, the Jew-hating blackshirt Oswald Mosley attended the college. In 2004 King Alfred's College became University College Winchester, enabling it to award its own degrees. Winchester has a population of 35,000 and a healthy student population, which keeps the city young and vibrant. Today, Winchester is a most welcoming, homely city that offers the freshness of the surrounding countryside - in fact, looking down from the Pentice, it is

possible to see the rolling countryside beyond. Winchester has many sophisticated and varied shops, making any shopping expedition a real treat. Only one hour from London, this is a near-perfect English city.

From Portsmouth's humble beginnings as a Saxon fishing village, it became a city in 1194 and gradually developed into the home of the Royal Navy. Portsmouth is renowned for its naval heritage and its harbour. Portsmouth's historic dockyard houses the great warships HMS 'Victory' and HMS 'Warrior'. King Henry VIII witnessed the sinking of his ship the 'Mary Rose' here. Portsmouth was the birthplace of Charles Dickens, and here Sherlock Holmes was created by Arthur Conan Doyle. Portsmouth has five museums, including Southsea Castle and the D-Day Museum that marks the 1944 Normandy landings. The city's spinnaker tower allows visitors to climb over 360ft and look across the south coast. Today, its population stands at 190,000. It is relatively quick and easy to sail from Portsmouth to France and Spain.

Southampton was declared a city in 1964, making it Hampshire's youngest city, yet there is much history here. In 1014, the Viking King Canute defeated King Ethelred in Southampton to become King of England. The town developed into one of the strongest fortresses in the land, and its wall measured up to 30ft high and incorporated twenty-nine towers and seven gates. In 1415, Henry V departed from here with his troops for France and the battle of Agincourt, after dealing with a treasonable plot. The traitors were tried and executed outside the Bargate, where their heads were displayed on spikes.

The Mayflower set sail for New England from Southampton in August 1620. From the 1750s to the 1800s Southampton enjoyed its status as a spa town; people flocked to drink from the mineral springs and bathe in the sea. The Prince of Wales bathed here in 1750 and Jane Austen visited in 1807, dancing the night away at the Dolphin Hotel. In 1879, horse-drawn trams were introduced to the town, and in 1898 they became electric. Trams left the town altogether in 1949.

The magnificent but ill-fated 'Titanic' sailed from Southampton docks on 10 April 1912. Then more tragedy struck in the Second World War, when German bombers reduced over 600 of Southampton's buildings to rubble, and damaged over 3,500 more. More than three million troops left from the docks for Normandy in the D-Day landings of 1944.

Southampton has played its part in vehicle production. The Gordon-Keeble GT 360bhp car was built here until 1967, and the ever-popular Ford Transit has been produced in Swaythling since the early 1970s. Today, Southampton is home to the University of Southampton, Southampton Institute, the Ordnance Survey and Southampton airport. Another landmark in the city's history was in 1976 when Southampton Football Club won the FA Cup. Southampton were following in the footsteps of Portsmouth, whose team had won the trophy in 1939.

This book concentrates on Hampshire between the 1940s and 1970s. The county's residents of the early to mid 1940s had the Second World War to contend with. There was the additional inconvenience of rationing; sweet rationing did not end until just before Coronation Day in 1953. Through the 1950s life slowly improved.

The 1960s were 'swinging', a happier decade with new fashions, new designs and new music – bands flourished, including the Troggs from Andover, who electrified the music scene with their hit single 'Wild Thing'; they performed at venues across the country, including the town hall in Basingstoke. Britain as a whole was prosperous in the 1960s, and so was Hampshire. Yet in 1965 there were more than three million people living in slums. The Government and local authorities built new homes. This was the era of high-rise flats, ugly houses and characterless shopping centres like the Tricorn centre in Portsmouth, built in the 1960s – many were thankful when it was demolished in 2004. Yet Hampshire has retained its character, and some Hampshire villages like Abbotts Ann and Goodworth Clatford have not changed.

In the 1960s supermarkets opened, and more women chose to work. A Hampshire man working in a factory was paid about £21 a week, but a woman was paid just £10 for doing the same work. The Equal Pay Act was passed in 1970, allowing women to be paid the same as men. Comprehensive schools were introduced to give all children the same opportunity. Society was more affluent, and people were able to buy fridges and freezers. 1967 saw foot and mouth disease spread across the country. In eight months, animals on over 2,000 farms contracted the disease and over 400,000 were slaughtered, a proportion of these in Hampshire.

Until 1970 Hampshire possessed only one motorway, the M3. This proved an immense boon to a number of places along the route of the old A30, notably Basingstoke, Camberley, and Hartley Wintney. After 1970 the M27 was constructed stretching from Christchurch to Brighton with twelve junctions. Before this, the traveller would have picked up the A303 that ran from Salisbury to London. Until 1974 both Bournemouth and Christchurch were part of Hampshire.

Not surprisingly, Hampshire's population has grown. There was no census in 1941 because of the Second World War, but in 1951 the population stood at almost 1,200,000; ten years later it had reached over 1,330,000. By 1971 the county's population exceeded 1,370,000. More people needed more houses. They needed employment to pay for those houses, and transport to get to work. These requirements were set to change Hampshire forever. Today, Hampshire's population exceeds 1,660,000.

Over its long history, Hampshire has been associated with a variety of influential characters. In the 20th century alone it has been linked with some well-known names in entertainment, architecture and design. Albert Hawthorne Hill was born in Eastleigh, Southampton in 1924 - his stage name was Benny Hill. Before the Second World War he was a milkman in the Swaythling area. He immortalised Eastleigh when he wrote a song about his time as a milkman and it reached No 1 in 1971: 'And he galloped into Market Street with his badge upon his chest. His name was Ernie, and he drove the fastest milk cart in the west'. Benny Hill could often be seen shopping in Bedford Place, Southampton.

Peter Sellers was born Richard Henry Sellers in Southsea in 1925. His parents called him Peter in memory of his stillborn older brother. Sellers's parents were vaudeville entertainers, and at two days old, Sellers was carried onto the stage at King's Theatre. He attended Miss Whitney's School of Dancing in Southsea.

In the 1960s the actor John Nettles read philosophy and history at Southampton University, where he also acted in drama society productions. He had a lucky break here, for he was spotted by an agent who arranged for him to work at the Royal Court Theatre.

A key performer until the mid 1960s was the legendary crooner Frankie Vaughan. His manager was Paul Cave, who has lived in Hampshire for over forty years and has done much to promote this fine county. He helped put the Bournemouth

WOOLSTON, *The Floating Bridge c1960* W468019

Winter Gardens on the map by introducing Morecambe and Wise there. Also, in 1960 he established 'HAMPSHIRE *the county magazine*', where he appointed Stirling Moss as its first motoring correspondent and John Arlott as a director and regular columnist. John Arlott was a true Hampshire hog with his strong Hampshire accent - he was born in Basingstoke. A well-known, friendly voice to scores of radio listeners, his cricket commentaries were unforgettable. John Arlott lived in Alresford for years until his death in the 1980s.

The architect Herbert Collins lived in Southampton from 1921 until his death in 1975. He designed distinctive housing estates in Southampton in the 1920s and 1930s. The Ministry of Health recognised his estates at Bassett Green and Uplands as good examples of housing design and layout. The houses were Georgian in style and two-storey, built of brick or rendered, with low-pitched clay or pantiled roofs.

His developments inspired the better council estates for about ten years after the Second World War.

The aircraft designer R J Mitchell designed many flying boats as well as the Spitfire. He lived in Swaythling before he died in 1937. The Spitfire played a major part in the Second World War, and with its stable mate the Hurricane it spelt the difference between victory and defeat. About 22,500 Spitfires were built. Sir Christopher Cockerell was another Hampshire designer; he brought the hovercraft into being, and his SRN1 became the world's first hovercraft. This was built by Saunders-Row on the Isle of Wight, and had a test run from Lee-on-the-Solent to Cowes in 1959.

There is much to remember about Hampshire's recent past. If you were not part of this era, it is hoped that you will glean a little of what the 1940s to the 1970s were like in this constantly evolving county. If you were part of it, then let us hope that this book will rekindle some memories.

HILL HEAD, *The Moorings c1955* H416005

HAMPSHIRE
LIVING MEMORIES

ABBOTTS ANN, *The Village c1955* A4006

A 1930s Rover saloon is parked on the road. A trout stream flows through the water meadow here. This village, three miles from Andover, is renowned for awarding virgins' crowns at the funerals of chaste villagers who were members of the village church and born here. The crowns are made of hazel twigs decorated with black and white paper rosettes and hung with five parchment gauntlets. The last crown was awarded in 1974.

▼ **ALDERSHOT,** *The Bathing Pool c1950* A31009

This was reputedly the largest and finest open-air bathing pool in the country. It covered ten acres, and contained well over one million gallons of water. Situated in the Aldershot Park estate (bought by the council in 1920 for £21,000), it was originally a lake; it was drained, and dressing rooms and lawns were added, costing £20,000. In 1948 the modern pentathlon of the XIV Olympiad was hosted here.

▶ **ALDERSHOT**
Union Street c1960
A31129

Parked outside Timothy Whites (left) is a 1954 Austin A40 Cambridge saloon. There were over 600 Timothy Whites chemists across the UK. In 1968, Timothy Whites was purchased by Boots, the self-service chemist. This premises is now a fashion shop. Today, Union Street is pedestrianised and home to many clothes shops and some antique shops. The occasional soldier can still be seen marching down the street.

◄ **ALTON**
Crown Hill c1955
A39097

The second shop down on the left at 55 High Street is Stoodley & Sons, the jewellers, established in 1861 and still trading in Alton today. Eight buildings down on the right is the Bakers Arms, and on its left is Kerridge's garage, demolished in 1963. The river still flows in a tunnel under the road and the buildings.

► **ALTON**
High Street c1955
A39003

The first building on the left is vacant, but it later became R E Goodfellow, a butcher's. This now allows access to the car park behind the manor house, some doors along. The post office is four doors down on the left. It still has a date stone of 1901 beneath the roof. The first car on the right is a 1956 Ford E83W Utility.

ALVERSTOKE
The Village c1955 A42003

This scene is largely unchanged today, with the lamp-post still pleasingly in the middle of the road, but there are road markings now. At No 47 was Alverstoke Antiques, cabinet makers and French polishers. The house on the left is no longer red brick. It would have been rendered not many years after this photograph was taken. In 1967, a new 4-bedroom house in nearby Gomer Lane cost £3,300.

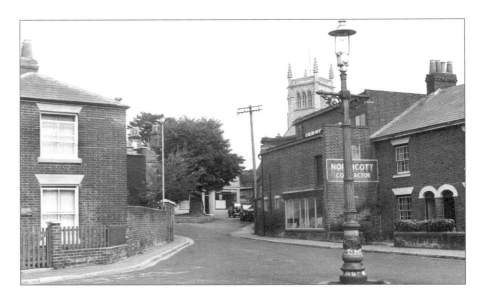

ANDOVER, *High Street c1955* A49069

Its name refers to its position on the river Anton. In 1945 its population was 16,000, but today it is three times that. High Street remains unchanged, and is still used for markets on Saturdays. Much of the northern half of the street is pedestrianised. Perhaps some of these cars came from Wessex Motors that sold Morris, MG, Riley, and Wolseley cars in nearby Bridge Street.

ANNA VALLEY
Tasker's Works c1955
A53008

This was the iron works that made such things as the bridge over Micheldever Road. About 900 people were employed here during the Second World War, when the firm manufactured aeroplane trailers large enough to carry aeroplanes for the RAF. The firm shut in 1968. Today modern housing can be found running alongside the river.

BARTON ON SEA, *The Village c1955* B690020

To the left of this photograph lies a golf course; over time more land has had to be purchased owing to erosion. In front of the chemist is a 1950 Daimler Consort saloon. The novelist Elizabeth Goudge lived with her parents in nearby Barton Lane. She wrote that Barton was 'a flat green plateau that is now a vast bungalow town'.

BARTON ON SEA

This mile-long beach is still pleasant in all seasons, especially the summer. From here there are views of the Isle of Wight. In 1970 a shop premises and living accommodation in Barton on Sea cost £27,500.

▶ **BASINGSTOKE**
Winchester Street
c1960 B31048

Basingstoke was bombed three times during the Second World War. Will the Austin A40 driver stop and buy some cigarettes from Hankin the tobacconist, the second shop on the left? Sally's, selling china and glass, the last shop on the right, is trading in Joice's Motor Coach Works where business ceased in 1950. Fire damaged the buildings in the 1960s. Today Winchester Street is pedestrianised.

◀ **BASINGSTOKE**
Market Place c1955 B31026

George Formby made a film here in 1944. Cars are parked by the town hall; it was home to the Galaxy Club from 1964 to 1966, and Screaming Lord Sutch and his Raving Savages, Lulu, and John Mayall's Blues Breakers featuring Eric Clapton, Mick Fleetwood, and John McVie all performed here. Fleetwood and McVie formed Fleetwood Mac. When the Spencer Davies Group performed here, tickets cost 7s 6d. Other performers were the Troggs from Andover and David Bowie. The Town Hall is now the Willis Museum. The Market Place is pedestrianised, and there is a market on Wednesdays and Saturdays. Lloyds Bank is still on the far left. The road with no entry signs (right) is Wote Street, home to the Haymarket Theatre.

▲ **BENTLEY,** *The Village c1955* B775005

To the right is the fresh new Triumph Herald 1200 coupe. It had a 25-foot turning circle. The A31 runs through the village, which stands between Farnham and Alton. Lord Baden-Powell, the Chief Scout, lived at Pax Hill from 1919 until his death in 1941; the house is now a nursing home. The Alice Holt forest is nearby.

◄ **BISHOP'S WALTHAM**
High Street c1955
B612068

The owners of these parked cars must be shopping. The first building on the left was Barclays Bank; today it is still Barclays, but it has had a fresh lick of paint. Houchin Street and Basingwell Street to the east of the High Street were cleared in the 1960s for car parks. H W Veck & Sons, a carpet retailer, has been trading here since 1928.

▶ **BISHOPSTOKE**
The Village
c1965 B693050

This village lies along the Itchen, where many old buildings can be found - the wide river fills one side of the road. Since the 1960s the village has expanded with new estates. To the south is a new development with its own shopping centre. Stoke Park Wood lies to the east of Bishopstoke.

▶ *(far right)detail from* B693050

◄ **BORDON**
The Village c1960
B143005

Well-controlled cows cross the quiet road. To the left, bicycles have been left unlocked leaning against a wall. Try doing that today expecting them to be there on your return! Now Bordon has grown to the size of a town. Two miles south is Woolmer Forest, and in the middle of it is the Army's Longmoor Camp.

BORDON
Chalet Hill c1960
B143036

This street has become estate agents' row - at Nos 4, 14, 18a and 24 Chalet Hill that is just what you will find. They have not taken over entirely, because there is a pet shop at No 10 and a hairdresser at No 20. The A325 Chalet Hill junction has a history of traffic accidents.

BOTLEY, *The Square c1955* B544011

Little has changed here today. There is a car park to the right, and traffic lights with a pedestrian crossing where the buses are in this photograph. Next to the Dolphin Hotel (left) is the pedimented market hall. Today there are a variety of shops here, ranging from specialist boutiques to a picture framer just down from the market hall. Behind the photographer is Botley Mills, which produced Botley self-raising flour.

BRAMLEY
The Village c1960
B696012

Today modern houses are interspersed with the cottages. Nearby, close to the church, older cottages with thatched roofs and latticed windows can be found. The eastern part of the village is more modern. Bramley Road to the south has an avenue of horse chestnut trees. The Army's Central Ammunition Depot was situated here - a sign for this can be seen in the Sherfield on Loddon photograph on page 92-93.

BRANSGORE, *The Crown Inn c1960* B695010

Perhaps the bicycle belongs to a customer who has nipped into this New Forest pub for a quick pint of Strong's best bitter. It must be a hot summer's day, because all of the windows are open. This pub was part of the Strong & Co group that controlled 215 inns. It employed 600 staff in and around Romsey, and its bitter appeared in almost every pub in the south of England. Strong's was taken over by Whitbread in 1969 and ceased trading in 1979. In April 1999 Hampshire Brewery re-launched Strong's best bitter. Today this pub belongs to Brewers Fayre, and has a children's' menu and disabled toilets - these would have been unavailable in 1960.

▲ **BROCKENHURST**
The Village c1955 B394007

Is the lady on the right expecting the two motorcyclists? Nearby, a Roman Catholic church was built in 1939. Hollands Wood is close to the village, and here there are pleasant ponds. There are attractive cottages in Brockenhurst, and some are thatched. Ash Cottage was the first village school; pupils paid 1d a week to attend. The Rose and Crown public house provided the village with its first bus service.

► *detail from* B394007

BUCKLER'S HARD
West Terrace c1960 B43057

What a picturesque village – today you must purchase a ticket to enjoy a visit here. A foal enjoys a well-earned rest, watched by two doting parents. The single street leads down to the river. An Austin A30 is parked beside an Armstrong Siddeley. Originally these 18th-century red brick cottages were for estate workers. The fifth cottage down from the start of the terrace, No 84, is a chapel, and No 74 is now the village shop. The last house

in the terrace was the master shipbuilder's house, now a pub. On the opposite side of the cottages is another almost identical row. Two and a half miles up the river is Beaulieu; boat trips are available, and upstream is a marina.

BURITON, *High Street c1960* B248011

Buriton is set in a wide valley. There are some flint cottages and malmstone cottages here, like the one on the left; we can see that brick has been used to surround the windows and doors – this is because malmstone is not as good quality as other stones. It seems that the thatch on this cottage has been recently repaired. Not far away is Queen Elizabeth Country Park.

▶ **BURLEY**
The Cricket Pitch
c1955 B647011

Not far from
Ringwood, Burley is
reputedly the jewel
in the crown of the
New Forest. These two
locals are standing
just in front of the
photographer, and
seem engrossed in
the cricket match.
Does one of them
own the car that the
lady is waiting in?
Nearby there is a
village school and a
couple of hotels,
Moorhill House
Hotel and Burley
Manor Hotel.

◀ **BURLEY**
The Village c1955
B647017

In the 1960s this New
Forest village was
home to a white witch
who roamed around
with a crow. A man is
hunched over his
parked car (right), no
doubt tinkering with
the engine. Further on
and to the left are a
family who might
have just popped into
Lloyds Bank to
withdraw some cash.
Are they going to
stroll still further to
the village stores?

▲ **BURSLEDON,** *The River Hamble c1960* B304007

To the right is the bridge over the river. Until the county council rebuilt it in the 1930s, tolls had to be paid to cross. Some houseboats were moored here for years; in the 1960s, residents enjoyed a peaceful existence, but now traffic thunders over the bridge. Boat owners can still moor up and hop ashore for a pint at the Jolly Sailor.

◀**CADNAM**
*The Sir John Barleycorn
c1960* C3012

Situated on Southampton Road, this is rumoured to be the oldest pub in Great Britain. Following a recent make-over, it now has slate and oak floors, leather furniture and oak tables. There is full table service in the non-smoking dining room with its inglenook. Not far from here is one of Hampshire's smallest waterways, the gravel-bottomed Cadnam River.

▶ **CHANDLER'S FORD**
Bournemouth Road
c1965 C490064

A lady pushes a pram towards the shops, while the man beside the Morris Minor (centre left) calls over the road to his wife. The second shop on the left is Lloyds Bank. Today the nearest branch of Lloyds TSB is in nearby Oakmount Road. In 1931 the population here was just over 3,000; now it is 20,000.

◀ **CHAWTON**
Jane Austen's House c1960
C530006

Chawton is two miles from Alton. The A31 changed to a local access road when the bypass was built in the 1970s, and Chawton is now bypassed completely. One longstanding local commented: 'On a summer's evening, I can now hear the steam trains on the Watercress Line - you couldn't when the A31 was here.' The black and white marks on the kerbstones in front of Jane Austen's house make drivers aware of the junction, increasing forward visibility. The black and white marks on the A31 sign, and the 30mph sign, were a requirement of the time, just as a grey pole is today. The 30mph speed limit was introduced in urban areas in 1935.

▲ **CHERITON,** *The Village c1955* C573007

Ducks sometimes swim on the river flowing through this charming village, which used to be renowned for truffle hunting. In 1975, a stone was erected marking the site of the Civil War battle of Cheriton that lies to the east of the village – the battle took place in 1644. In the village centre is the church of St Michael and All Angels. Some of the stained glass was given in memory of men killed in the First World War.

◄ **CHURCH CROOKHAM**
The Crossroads c1960
C102028

Left takes you to Fleet and right to Farnham. Is the lady going to catch a bus to Farnham? The first car on the left seems to be parked on the bend; the driver might have got away with this in 1960, but today this would be highly irresponsible. On both sides of the road the white lines seem to go past the central reservation – this would not be so today.

◀ **COWPLAIN**
The Shopping Parade
c1960 C576029

A lady makes a phone call in the red telephone box. These were installed all over the UK in the 1950s. Cowplain developed because of the main road from Portsmouth to London; its name means 'a clearing for cows'. It is not far from the Forest of Bere, where there are plenty of oak trees, like those on the right of this photograph.

◀ **CLANFIELD**
The Rising Sun
c1955 C574004

There are still some swift pints to be enjoyed at this pub in North Lane; Watneys were London-based brewers. Clanfield sits in a valley to the west of the A3, 12 miles north of Portsmouth, and 6 miles south of Petersfield. Its name derives from Old English, and means 'field clean of weeds'. In 1929 its population was 129, in the 1940s it was 500, and in 1998 it was 4,500, with over 1,700 houses.

▲ **CRONDALL,** *The Village c1950* C194002

Here, over 80 listed buildings are surrounded by picturesque farmland. Until 1935 there was a hand-pumped fire engine in the village. The school shut in 1945, and the pub disappeared in 1950. Nearby lived Denis Jenkinson, the racing driver who in 1955 had partnered Stirling Moss in a Mercedes Benz to win the Mille Miglia, that fearsome 1,000-mile race running from Brescia to Rome. The race was stopped in 1957.

◀ **DENMEAD**
The Green 1960
D181013

Since the Second World War this village has grown. Situated on the B2150 between Waterlooville on the A3 and Droxford on the A32, it is only 20 minutes from Portsmouth and 30 minutes from Southampton. Today it has a population of over 6,000. There are a variety of shops here, including Denmead Village News and Denmead Post Office within the One-Stop convenience store.

▼ **DIBDEN PURLIEU,** *Merrimead Parade c1960* D196003

These shops are beside Beaulieu Road. C M Topp the grocer (far left) is still trading. There was also a newsagent here. Just off the main street in North Road is the Methodist church. Some of the village shops were built from corrugated iron before modernisation in the early 1960s. Richard Eurich RA, the official war artist to the Admiralty from 1941, lived here.

► **DOWNTON**

The Royal Oak c1960
D197028

This pub can still be found on Christchurch Road in Downton, near Lymington. The tree looks too near the pub for comfort, but it is still there today. Some subtle changes have occurred: the top windows now have wooden shutters, there are porches over both front doors, the planters have disappeared, and, of course, Strong & Co no longer manage this pub.

◄DRAYTON
Havant Road c1955
D224017

Rows of black cars line the sides of the road. Today there are estate agents, an optometrist and a surgery here; the surgery dates from 1937 when Dr Cheyne opened it in his Havant Road home. The practice moved to No 274 in 1957. This building was extended but was still too small, so the new Drayton Surgery was constructed in 1996 at No 280.

► DROXFORD
High Street c1960
D198008

The scenic A32 runs through Droxford, which lies between Alton and Gosport. The first shop on the left is the post office – it has now moved. Next door is the Bakers Arms pub; in 1961 it was taken over by Mr and Mrs Calder-Smith. At that time the soup of the day cost 1s 6d and a gammon with pineapple main course was 9s 6d. This pub is still trading.

▶ **EAST MEON**
The River c1955
E173014

The fencing on either side of the river has now been painted white. In the distance, the telegraph pole and phone box have been removed. There is now a monument with a cross at the top, to the left, where the telephone box was. In 1965 one of the two-bedroom cottages beside the river sold for £2,350; it would now cost £235,000.

▶ *(far right) detail from* E173014

▼ *(below) detail from* E167020

◄ EASTLEIGH
High Street c1960 E167020

In 1936 Eastleigh became a borough. This photograph was taken looking north up the High Street. To the left is Market Street, now pedestrianised, to the right is Blenheim Road, and behind the photographer is the park. No 39 High Street was Clemoes, a women's wear shop, now a pizza parlour. The first and second shop on the right was Delbridges. Today these premises are restaurants. The third shop down was John Cole, a furniture shop that is now an interiors shop. Half way down on the right is Eastleigh Museum. The no entry sign has been removed, and traffic now goes down this street but not up, as in this photograph. Behind the oncoming bus is the Swan Centre. Eastleigh's population is now 55,000.

ELING, *The Quay c1955* E252022

Here boats are moored on the estuary of Eling Creek with its causeway and centuries-old toll bridge. The causeway encloses water for Eling Tide Mill, visible in the distance. This worked until 1941, and was restored and opened as a museum in 1980. Eling still remains a village, while neighbouring areas like Totton and Copythorne do not.

EMERY DOWN
The Swan Inn c1960
E196013

The Swan Inn is south of Lyndhurst. A turning to the A35 is opposite it, and here we find Leominstead Lakes, where trout fishing is available daily. The village of Emery Down is reached by turning right at Swan Green after leaving Lyndhurst on the A35 Bournemouth road. There are plenty of oak trees, foxgloves and thatched cottages in this pretty New Forest village.

EMSWORTH, *The Square c1955* E62013

Today St Peter's Square is home to several coffee shops as well as the new Emsworth library, a butcher's, and a baker's that makes delicious cheesecakes. There is also a greengrocer, a newsagent, bookshops and several estate agents. Nearby is Emsworth marina, which was created in 1964 from a log pond.

▼ **EXTON,** *Church View Cottages c1955* E221017

Nos 1 and 2 Church View Cottages were built in the 17th century. They are good examples of timber-framed houses with brick in-fill and casement windows. Today, owing to the expense of replacing thatch, both cottages have slate roofs. Not far from here the River Meon passes by Exton church.

► **FAIR OAK**
*Eastleigh Road
c1965* F164003

The cyclist is about to overtake a dented Morris 8 saloon. Nearby is the church graveyard. When it became full, a new cemetery opened in 1942, and Mr Latimer was appointed as gravedigger; it is ironic that he died before he could start work and was the first person to be buried there. Today the parish of Fair Oak incorporates Horton Heath, and its population is now over 8,000.

◀ **FAREHAM**
West Street c1955 F103017

A Ford Consul heads out of Fareham. West Street is a mile long, and this section is now pedestrianised. The clock (centre left) has been removed, a line of trees has been planted to the right, and there are some benches for weary shoppers. On the right, just behind where the lorry is parked, there is now a shopping precinct. There are still a variety of shops to be found here. On the left where the cars are parked is Westbury Manor Museum, which has installed iron sculptures in the town centre around West Street. This was done to celebrate the millennium and the life of Henry Cort, who lived on the outskirts of Fareham. He pioneered a method of forging iron during the Industrial Revolution.

▶ **FARNBOROUGH**
Queens Mead Shopping Centre c1965 F9156

Farnborough is home to much modern architecture; some might say it was bland and characterless. There are three massive shopping centres here. One of these is Queens Mead, which is home to over 80 shops. There are 600 parking spaces here, and the railway station is less than a mile away, making Farnborough useful to London commuters.

FAWLEY
The Falcon Inn
c1955 F150008

This is a good example of Art Deco design. Fawley is home to the Esso oil refinery, which lies to the south of the parish; it started operating in 1951, and covers 3,000 acres. All Saints' Church stands beside the entrance to the refinery, and it was bombed during the Second World War. In 1971 the Fawley power station started generating electricity.

FLEET
Fleet Road c1965
F32029

This road is the main shopping street in Fleet, and it contains a mixture of architecture from Victorian to modern. Fleet is only 40 miles from London, and is located next to Aldershot and Farnborough; the Basingstoke Canal runs across the town. Today the population stands at 26,000. Not far from here is Fleet Pond, more of a lake than a pond.

FORDINGBRIDGE, *The Village c1960* F178034

The local policeman (centre) goes on his daily beat around this peaceful village – a sight not to be seen now. The nearby River Avon attracts anglers. Augustus John, the painter, lived at Fryern Court, north of the village, from 1927 to 1961. St Mary's Church is to the south of the village, and the stained glass in the north chapel was added in the 1970s.

FROXFIELD GREEN
The Green c1960
F188021

On a clear day you can see the sea from here. This Hampshire village has many trees, windy roads, and the occasional hill. Time has treated this peaceful area well. There are some fine cottages here, and no new housing. Since 1924, Froxfield has been home to the Edward Barnsley workshop; it makes superb furniture, and has its roots in the Arts and Crafts movement.

FULLERTON, *Cottage on the Bridge c1960* F109001

What a lovely view can be had from this thatched cottage. The occasional vehicle will be heard from inside, but apart from that, it is a peaceful life here. As the water flows underneath the bridge the occasional fish can be seen. At Fullerton the River Test meets the River Anton and then passes Stockbridge and Romsey to enter Southampton Water.

▼ **GOODWORTH CLATFORD,** *The Village c1965* G87014

This is another picturesque Hampshire village, home to a good selection of perfect whitewashed thatched cottages. Even today, this is a sleepy village removed from the hustle and bustle of busy town life. It is not difficult to hear birds happily chirping here, unlike in our busy towns. The church of St Peter can be found on one side of the river.

▶ **GRAYSHOTT**
Headley Road c1960
G48041

Most cars on our roads used to be British; the first one, just visible on the left here is a Morris Minor, and the second is a Rover 75. The second shop on the left is a hairdresser's - there are many of these to choose from today, and there is also a butcher and a chemist. Grayshott's buildings date from the 19th and 20th centuries. The Hampshire/Surrey border boundary stone stands on this road.

◀ HAMBLE
The Harbourside c1955
H148003

The annual sailing regatta declined in the 1920s. New crowd-pulling ideas included carnivals and processions. In the 1960s formation sailing was performed by the light of coloured searchlights. Today, Hamble Week promotes local produce. In 1936, Hamble became home to the Royal Southern Yacht Club that had moved from Southampton town quay. Then, during the Second World War, X-craft midget submarines were assembled on the Hamble; these 50-foot craft attacked German battleships. The war halted all yachting, with yachtsmen being called up. To the right of this photograph, it is still possible to catch the small pink Hamble ferry to Warsash. The National Provincial Bank (right) is not here today. In the 1970s a 5-bedroom property near Hamble River cost £40,000.

▶ HAMBLEDON
High Street c1955
H405014

When we look at this photograph, our eyes are instantly drawn to the church in the distance. Few people owned a car at this time. It looks as if the Ford Zephyr on the right has an L-plate on its bumper - perhaps the owner of the house is learning to drive. At this time, red telephone boxes like the one on the right were a common sight.

▲ **HARTLEY WESPALL**
*The Post Office and Stores
c1960* H370009

This pleasant village has a farm
and a church. The rest of the
village is to the south. The driver
of the Triumph Herald 1200
patiently waits, with his window
wound down, for his wife to post
a letter and buy a newspaper. In
1965 a brand new one of these,
complete with walnut fascia, cost
£592-8s-9d at Sparshatts, Castle
Way, Southampton.

▶ *detail from* H370009

HARTLEY WINTNEY
High Street c1965
H247048

This village today has a population of 5,000. It retains a distinctly rural character, yet also has the attributes of a small town with shops on either side of the road. Probably the oldest shop is A W Porter & Son: established in 1844, it is a jeweller's, a clockmaker's, a silversmith's and an antique dealer's.

HAVANT, *East Street c1955* H147035

Just before the Bear Hotel (left), which is still trading today, is a crossroads where South Street and East Street meet. The buildings in Havant are generally Georgian, and some good examples can still be found here. Today the varied selection of shops down this street includes a ski shop. Havant Arts Centre and Havant Museum are also to be found here.

HAWKLEY
The Village c1960
H424004

Spectacular countryside views can be enjoyed here. This village lies around a green, and here the church of St Peter and St Paul can be found. At the first house on the right, a window beside the front door has been bricked up. Many cottages here are brick, and there are also some malmstone ones. A couple (centre left) stroll through the village; their clothing suggests that it is a warm day.

HAWLEY, *Randell House c1955* H50011

Randell House was previously called All Saints' Home; it housed young homeless children from London slums until 1937, when it became a house of rest and prayer for ladies. At the outbreak of the Second World War it closed for a short time. The home was handed over to the Royal United Kingdom Beneficent Association in 1953, who modernised it. It is now run as a charitable senior citizens' residence.

HAYLING ISLAND
Mengham Road c1965
H400031

Hayling is linked to the mainland by a concrete road bridge that opened in 1956, replacing the wooden toll bridge. In the 1930s the toll was 8d for a car, quite expensive at a time when a craftsman earned 1s 2d per hour. In 1933 nine Hayling coastguard cottages plus a building plot were sold for £3,280, and in 1965 a 4-bedroom house with garden and garage in Hayling cost £10,500. Hayling's women's hockey club was formed in

1935. In 1938 the Regal cinema opened in Mengham Road, but it was demolished in the 1960s, and in its place is Mengham car park. In 1959 Hayling's population was 6,000; today it has tripled. The Hayling Billy train ran during the summer, and was packed with passengers, but the railway shut in 1964.

HEADLEY DOWN, *The Post Office c1955* H415009

This is a relatively modern development, while a mile and half away is the older village of Headley. There are still plenty of trees here. The church has a peal of six bells, given in 1935 in the memory of Mr and Mrs McAndrew, who donated the village hall to the Women's Institute. Nearby, Headley Mill is still working, and is a popular beauty spot.

▶ **HILL HEAD**
The Moorings
c1955 H416005

Not far from Lee-on-the-Solent, this is a wonderful spot for sailing. Is the man on the right about to set sail? The road leads all the way round the shore here, and today there is a car park behind the third building. To the west, the left of this photograph, lies 1,000 acres of farmland that is managed as a nature reserve.

▶ *(far right) detail from* H416005

◀ **HOLYBOURNE**
Main Road c1960
H104003

Underneath this main road flows a stream that rises from a spring under the church of the Holy Rood, built in the 12th century. The village takes its name from this stream that joins the River Wey at Neatham. Perhaps the couple pushing the pram on the right are making their way home for a warm cup of tea - the lady's attire suggests that it is cold.

◀ *(far left) detail from* H416003

▼ **HOOK,** *London Road c1955* H385006

A cyclist wisely waits for the lorry before he rides across the road. Hook had a 'tin tabernacle' church until 1938, when it was replaced. In the 1960s, housing estates emerged everywhere, and Hook was to be no exception. Until this time growth had been gradual; now it has soared.

▶ **HORNDEAN**
The Village c1955 H403016

The cream-washed, plaster-faced pub on the right belonging to Gales brewery is the Ship & Bell. This former coaching inn stands on London Road, the old London to Portsmouth road. Next door is Gales brewery, whose brewing tower dominates the rooftops of Horndean. Today Gales owns over 100 public houses.

◄ HURSTBOURNE TARRANT
The Village
c1955 H417014

This picturesque village featured in Anna Lea Merritt's book 'A Hamlet in Old Hampshire', published in 1902, describing 19th-century village life. When Anna died in 1930, a memorial was placed in the local church. Thatched cottages in the village line the occasionally-running stream that meanders through the lovely landscape.

► HYTHE
High Street
c1955 H372039

Until the 1950s, Hythe was the maintenance base for Southampton's flying boats. This area has expanded greatly since the end of the Second World War. Here, a man looks thoughtfully in the shop window on the left.

HYTHE
The Ferry c1960 H372077

The 'Hotspur III' was launched at the end of January 1938. It joined 'Hotspur I' and 'Hotspur II' running from Southampton to Hythe every half an hour during the day. They would drop and collect passengers from the pier, where an electric railway connected to the mainland. In July 1952, 50,000 people crammed onto the pier to witness the world's fastest liner and Blue Riband voyage winner, the 'United States', arrive in Southampton.

▶ **IBSLEY**
The Old Beams
c1955 I55003

Thatch and timber buildings such as the one in this photograph are not an uncommon sight in Ibsley. There is a small brick church here, as well as a stone bridge over the river to Harbridge. Not far away is Moyles Court, a school, and between here and Ibsley there are some lakes.

◀**KEYHAVEN**
The Harbour c1955
K146003

An artist (left) settles down to capture some of this marvellous scenery on canvas. A small selection of boats can be seen moored here. The marshes are home to large populations of birds that include wild fowl, little terns, and black-headed gulls. In the summer, ferries regularly run to Hurst Castle, and there are boats to the Isle of Wight.

▲ **KINGS SOMBORNE,** *The Village c1955* K99002

Could the dog be waiting for his weary owner to catch up? This village is close to the Test Valley. There are many thatched cottages to be enjoyed here. At this time it was common policy to destroy dilapidated buildings rather than repair them. Consequently, some character has gone from this village, but there is still a pub, a church and a few shops.

◄ **KINGSCLERE**
Market Place c1960 K140073

There are grey and red brick buildings here. The cottages straight ahead were built in the 1860s. On the left is the Crown Inn, where a gruesome event took place in 1944. US Army units were based around here, and ten US soldiers walked into the Crown and got drunk. Two US military police asked them for their passes. When they failed to produce these, the ten men stormed back to camp, helping themselves to rifles. On returning to the Crown they checked that the policemen were still inside and then opened fire, killing them and Mrs Napper, the landlord's wife. Nine of the soldiers were charged with murder and given life imprisonment. The tenth was discharged from the Army and given ten years hard labour.

▼ **LANGSTONE,** *The Harbour c1955* L481009

Virtually unchanged today, the Royal Oak pub (left background) is still trading. The elves on their toadstools in the foreground have disappeared - a life-saving device now stands on the spot between where the two elves once were. It seems a little odd to see a windmill so near the shore. The author and aeronautical engineer Neville Shute lived here between 1934 and 1940 when he worked at Portsmouth Airport.

▶ **LEE-ON-THE-SOLENT**
Lee Tower c1955
L461005

Lee Tower was built at the end of the pier in 1935; it was Art Deco in style, and 120 ft tall. From the top it was possible to see right across the Solent to the Isle of Wight. Inside there was a restaurant, a cinema and reputedly the south coast's best ballroom. Unfortunately, it was pulled down in 1971. Lee has definitely lost some of its character.

LEPE
The Beach c1955
L482014

Here we see a busy day in the summer. Girls watch the boys go by. Fashions have changed: there are no bikinis and no bare chests here. This is still a sandy beach on the Solent shore; many beaches in Hampshire are now pebble, possibly due to erosion. There are stunning views over the Solent to the Isle of Wight from here. In the 1970s a six-bedroom property with staff cottage in Lepe cost £70,000.

▶ **LINDFORD**
The Village c1955
L341001

On the left was the shop that included the post office. Inside, you could buy almost anything: there was paraffin, bacon, and butter in a glass cabinet, and sweets in glass jars. The previous owners were bakers, but the bakehouse in the garden was pulled down. Opposite is the pub. Bottled milk was delivered to villagers' doorsteps by Mr Souter, the milkman.

LIPHOOK
The Village c1955
L52017

All looks peaceful and quiet in this photograph. Today all roads seem to lead into Liphook, and it is a busy, noisy place. The author Flora Thompson lived here for a time just before the 1930s because her husband worked at the local post office. She wrote part of her book 'Lark Rise to Candleford' here.

LISS, *Station Road c1955* L54005

The first parked car on the left is a 1946 Morris Eight Series E Saloon. It has recently rained, but the shadows suggest that the sun is coming out. A baby girl waits in her pram for her mother to come out of the first shop on the right. The Railway Hotel in the distance is still trading. Today's shops include a butcher's and a newsagent's.

LOCKERLEY
Butts Green c1955
L367026

A boy runs across to meet his friend by the large green on the left. Perhaps they are going to meet some more friends and play a game of tag. This pleasant, peaceful and picturesque area has some cottages scattered about and little else. There is a stone church close to the nearby railway line.

LYMINGTON, *The Ferry c1955* L148019

A 1947 Humber Hawk makes its way off the ferry. The ferry still runs from Lymington to Yarmouth on the Isle of Wight, and takes 30 minutes. Ferry ownership passed from the British Railways Board to Sealink UK Ltd, and the service is now provided by Wightlink. The two marinas in Lymington are at the ferry terminal and at the town quay, which has room for 100 boats.

LYMINGTON
High Street c1955 L148091

The fourth building on the right used to be blue, and it still is. Then it was Batemans Opticians; now it is a boutique. Next but one was Smith the chemist's - the projecting sign is now removed. F C Webb's shoe shop was seventh along, and above it was a hairdresser's. Today there is a photo developer and an osteopath's. Now the pavement is indented to include a bus stop, and there is a pedestrian crossing and road markings.

LYNDHURST
High Street c1955
L123030

The buildings here have not changed much, although the garage on the right is no longer there. There is a Maserati car dealership at the end of the High Street. The road system has changed: today there is a one-way system where cars travel down the High Street towards Beaulieu, Southampton, Brockenhurst and Christchurch. In the summer, traffic is nose to tail because of the traffic lights.

LYNDHURST, *The Grand Hotel c1955* L123039

Today this is the Lyndhurst Park Hotel. Its address is 78 High Street, and it is Forestdale Hotels' head office. They have purchased nineteen 3-star hotels in England and France over the last 38 years. This elegant Georgian mansion, set within three acres, is surrounded by the 90,000 acres of the New Forest where ponies roam free. Rooms are priced from £45 upwards.

MEDSTEAD
The Post Office c1955
M324022

This post office and hardware shop is near to the church of St Andrew, the church hall that was previously the village school, and the Castle of Comfort pub. In 1966 Medstead's population was 1,200, and today it is 2,000. East of Winchester, it is one of the highest villages in Hampshire, 700 ft above sea level. There are some magnificent views to be enjoyed from here.

MEONSTOKE, *Bucks Head Hill c1955* M304018

Perhaps the motorcyclist is riding to Corhampton, quarter of a mile away, but he must watch out for the stray cow in the distance. He is next to Church End Cottages, which are timber-framed with hipped tiled roofs. The popular Bucks Head pub is on the right. Cows are being herded up the hill towards the triangular green, where there is a road running southwards.

▶ **MICHELDEVER**
The Village c1955 M177010

The sun is shining on another outstanding Hampshire village with some timeless timber-framed cottages and nicely cut hedges. The broadcaster Sir David Frost is rumoured to live here. Here we see good examples of black and white half-thatched cottages with brick nogging between the timbers that has been painted. Unfortunately, this village is affected by the unrepentant roar of traffic from the A33 and the M3 and by the trains.

▶ *(far right) detail from* M177010

◀ **MIDDLE WALLOP**
The Crossroads c1955
M272002

In the middle of Over and Nether Wallop, the river runs beside the road. To the north-east lies the Second World War airfield which has been the centre for army flying since 1958. Today, there is a museum here tracing the history of army flying and helicopter development since the 1940s. There is also an air show here every few years.

MILFORD ON SEA
The Village c1955
M303091

Milford developed into a seaside resort in the 19th century, and there are many Victorian and Edwardian houses and bungalows. In 1960 a new 3-bedroom bungalow with a garage and two WCs cost £4,700. Not long after this photograph was taken, flats became popular, and today there are unsightly blocks of flats on the outskirts of this village. From here there are superb views of Hengistbury Head, the Isle of Wight and Hurst Castle.

▼ **MILFORD ON SEA,** *High Street c1960* M303158

The sun is out in Milford today. Straight ahead, W B Mew Langton & Co Ltd are receiving a delivery. A Mini is parked outside the Red Lion pub on the right. Does it belong to the barmaid? Today there are a variety of shops in Milford on Sea, ranging from a convenience store to a hairdresser's.

▶ **NETHER WALLOP**
The Square c1955
N156001

Perhaps this villager is heading towards O J Hinwood, to fill up his petrol can. You do not see petrol pumps like the ones outside the shop any more. This picturesque village has cottages lining its winding streets, and the trickling sound of water can be heard from the river. This remains a nice village in which to enjoy a walk.

◀ **NETLEY**
The Royal Victoria Hospital c1955 N10018

At 1,424 ft long, this was one of the world's longest buildings; it was the first and the largest army hospital. The hospital is now demolished, and today this is the site of Royal Victoria Country Park. Only the chapel survives, which is now a museum. The tower can be accessed, and it gives a wide view of Southampton Water. Behind the hospital ran the railway, and some rails remain.

▶ **NETLEY**
The Castle c1965
N10080

The castle stands opposite Netley Abbey; most of the surrounding area has now been filled with housing. This extravagant building is located on the shore; it mostly dates from the late 19th century. In the middle is a block built by Henry VIII in 1542 as a small fort opposite Calshot Castle.

▶ **NEW MILTON**
High Street
c1965 N58048

The town centre is in the distance; there are some Edwardian and many modern buildings here. To the north is a pond, and south of the railway line is a water tower resembling a castle. To the west is the Sammy Miller Museum that displays motorcycles. The exclusive Chewton Glen Hotel is nearby; it started trading in the 1960s, and many film stars have stayed here.

◀ **NEWTOWN**
Ye Swan Inn c1955 N197006

Situated in North Hampshire, on the border with Berkshire, Ye Swan Inn is the first Hampshire building to be seen when coming south. Still sparsely populated, Newtown does not feel large enough to be a village, although it does have a church, dedicated to St Mary and St John Baptist. There is plenty of woodland here.

▲ **NORTH WARNBOROUGH,** *The Jolly Miller c1955* N198002

The Jolly Miller on Hook Road has a skittles evening each week. It has ten bedrooms, all with televisions - they would not have had these in 1955. A single bedroom costs £39 including breakfast. Odiham and North Warnborough have a combined population of 4,700. Approximately 45 miles west of London, North Warnborough is not far from junction 5 of the M3. Nearby railway stations are Hook and Winchfield.

◀ **OAKLEY**
The Post Office c1955
O111021

This post office is at 22 Oakley Lane, and is still trading today. Since the 1960s, Oakley has grown considerably, and its population is now 7,000. This village is just outside Basingstoke, and at its centre is the pond with its family of ducks. It is here that the annual Christmas carol concert is held every year. There are three churches in Oakley.

ODIHAM
*The George Hotel and
High Street c1955* 08041

These were the days when
Morris Minors were a
common sight. Odiham's
High Street has a variety of
shops, and its buildings date
from between the
16th and 19th centuries.
The second building on the
left is the George Hotel,
which is still trading. Odiham
is also home to an art gallery
and Barclays Bank. Little has
changed here.

OLD BURSLEDON
The Post Office c1965
O112042

The sun highlights the front of the post office on this quiet, peaceful road. A bicycle leans against the wall. Strawberry growing was still a popular occupation around here. The lanes were quiet and occasional horse-drawn vehicles might be seen. The post office was also the local shop and delivered bread, groceries, meat and milk to many villagers' doorsteps; now it is a private house.

OVER WALLOP, *Station Road c1965* O98002

Next to the thatched cottages on the left is the White Hart pub. We can see thatched cob walls on both the left and the right; Over Wallop is the place to go in Hampshire to see this regional speciality. Middle, Nether and Over Wallop line the Wallop Brook that joins the River Test above Bossington.

OVERTON
The Greyhound, Winchester Street c1955 O40027

A family pack up their car to go on holiday. At 46 Winchester Street, the Greyhound belonged to Simonds Brewery in Reading that owned many pubs. It brewed Simonds Golden Dry Export that was popular at the time. This brewery was taken over by Courage. The Greyhound still serves pints today, and has live music. It stands near Overton railway station.

PETERSFIELD, *High Street c1965* P48078

The first shop on the right is Boots at No 10. Next door is Woolworths, and next but one is Westminster Bank at No 4. These three businesses are still in Petersfield at the same addresses. Today, at the back of 16 High Street lies Petersfield Physic Garden. In 1961 Petersfield's population was 7,000, while today it is 14,000.

PETERSFIELD
The Market Place
c1955 P48039

What an array of
now classic cars;
today, you would
pay to see these at
Beaulieu Motor
Museum. Petersfield
is a true market
town, for markets
are still held here
on Wednesdays and
Saturdays. To the
left is a pub; the
third building along
in the distance is
Lloyds Bank, and
next to it is the
Square Brewery.
Little has changed,
apart from new
businesses trading
here.

▼ **PILLEY,** *The Post Office c1955* P285003

Pilley is one of six hamlets making up Boldre in the New Forest. The others are Bailey, Bull Hill, Portmore, Sandy Down, Walhampton, and Boldre itself. When every home did not have a telephone, the telephone box beside the post office offered access to the outside world, and so did the red post box. In addition, the post office was the social hub of many villages.

▶ **PORTCHESTER**
Castle Street c1960
P73016

A mother and her two sons head home (right). Since the 1930s thousands of houses have been built in Portchester. The A27 is at one end of Castle Street. From the White Hart pub to the castle there are a variety of Georgian red brick properties. There is a small green where an oak tree was planted marking the 1935 Jubilee. Portchester has a railway station.

◀ **PORTSMOUTH**
The Jetty, the Sally Port
c1955 P100067

In April 1956, Commander Lionel Crabb, Britain's finest frogman, disappeared whilst diving at Stokes Bay, Gosport. On 17 April, Mr Crabb had stayed overnight at the Sallyport Hotel in Old Portsmouth. That evening Crabb went to Havant and caught a train back to Portsmouth. A frogman was seen entering the sea at the mouth of Portsmouth harbour. A Mr Smith settled Crabb's hotel bill and removed Crabb's possessions. Plain-clothes police officers tore out the details of everyone staying at the hotel on 17 April. Fourteen months later, three fishermen discovered what was believed to be Crabb's corpse in Chichester harbour. It is still a mystery whether Crabb drowned, was shot, or was kidnapped. In 1965 the 'Mary Rose' was discovered at Portsmouth harbour.

▶ **PRESTON CANDOVER**
Canterton Stores
c1960 P166049

In the days when supermarkets were uncommon, Canterton Stores would have provided villagers with almost everything they required. In the middle of Preston Candover is the Victorian church, St Mary's. There are two large Georgian houses and some nicely thatched cottages. It is still a peaceful village, although there is more traffic.

▼ **PURBROOK,** *The White Hart c1960* P340006

Does the Morris Minor belong to the landlord? This pub was owned by Brickwood, the Portsmouth brewery. They brewed Sunshine IPA, Pompey XXXXX Dark Ale, and Admiral Stout. In the 1960s their advertisements often showed a jovial man holding a pint and a caption reading 'Drop in for a while at the pub with a smile'.

► **RINGWOOD**

High Street c1950 R35017

Ringwood sits on the River Avon, and is situated on the Hampshire/Dorset border. In 1936 the town mill was demolished, making way for the first Ringwood bypass - it has since been widened. The fifth building on the left is Woolley & Wallis the estate agents, who are still trading. In 1961 in nearby Market Place, Ringwood Electrical sold the new vapour-controlled Russell Hobbs kettle for £6 1s.

◀ ROMSEY
Market Place c1965
R53062

To the right at 27 Market Place is the post office. In July 1965 this was transformed into the Westminster Bank, where Mr Gambrill was the manager - he had been with the bank for 31 years. Boots is still here, and there is a regular market. In 1956 Norman Thelwell, the world-renowned cartoonist who had produced 60 covers and 1,500 illustrations for 'Punch' magazine, moved to Braishfield near Romsey, where he gained a reputation for exemplary property restoration. In 1968 the Thelwells moved to nearby Timsbury where Thelwell fulfilled a lifetime ambition by building a lake close to his beloved River Test.

▶ ROWLAND'S CASTLE
The Stores and the Railway Hotel c1965
R83044

We can assume that it is winter by the look of the tree. A lady waits for her husband beside their car. Has he leaned an item of furniture against the telephone box? Three buildings along is the Railway Hotel. Rowlands Castle, on the Sussex border, is named after the medieval castle that had been destroyed by the building of the railway running from London to Portsmouth.

SARISBURY GREEN
The Parade c1965
S629053

Newbury & Sons (left) is now a convenience store. The post office on the left shut in 2004. Parked is a Hillman Imp with L-plates that in 1967 cost £665 at Alec Bennett in Portswood. The building with the rooftop rail beyond Newbury's is Sarisbury Buildings. The New Inn on the end changed its name to the Sarisbury, but it shut in 2004, to be converted into flats.

▶ **SELBORNE**
High Street c1960
S89030

When Selborne is
seen from Selborne
Hanger on a
summer's day it
looks absolutely
spectacular, a typical
Hampshire village.
It has suffered from
heavy lorries
rumbling through;
now, those over
7.5 tonnes have
been banned.
There are two
thriving pubs; one of
them, the Queen's
Hotel, is on the left.
There are shops, a
post office, a village
hall and a sports
pavilion.

▶ *(far right) detail
from* S89030

◀ **SHERFIELD ON LODDON**
The White Hart c1965
S631020

The sign in the foreground points to the Army's Central Ammunitions Depot in Bramley Road, which eventually shut in the 1970s. Straight ahead is the White Hart, an 18th-century colour-washed brick building. Still trading, it has toothed eaves and an old tiled roof. Inside, above the fireplace, there are rare pigeon holes for mail. Sherfield on Loddon is 5 miles from the M3.

◀ *(far left) detail from*
S631020

SILCHESTER, *The Clock c1965* S632028

In the north of the county sits Silchester. This modern clock tower is part of Silchester House, built in 1820, but the clock tower is more modern. Silchester House is an attractive gabled rambling building with decorative chimneys. It is stuccoed - a fine plaster has been used for coating the walls. Two Roman soldiers hold the bell - appropriate for this town which was a Roman settlement.

SOUTH TIDWORTH
Old Cottages c1955
S633009

South Tidworth is situated in the Test Valley, but in the 1974 boundary changes it ended up in Wiltshire. These thatched cottages are by the old Reading Room on the North and South Tidworth borders. In front of the Reading Room is a red telephone box. To the left of the telephone box is the Royal Ordnance depot that issued clothing and equipment to Army personnel.

SOUTH WARNBOROUGH, *The Village and the War Memorial c1955* S634014

The village's name comes from 'weargebuman', a Saxon word meaning 'white water' or 'felon stream'. The village, with its church of St Andrew, retains many old thatched brick and half-timbered cottages, along with a village shop. Southwards, between the River Whitewater and the North Downs, the land rises to 700 ft, one of the highest points in Hampshire. The countryside is unspoilt.

▼ **SOUTHAMPTON,** *Bargate c1955* S151013

This was Southampton's main entrance until the 1930s. In 1961, a box of three Irish linen hand-rolled handkerchiefs cost 8s 11d from Bourne & Hollingsworth in the Bargate. At 12 Bargate, University Cameras (they also sold hi-fis) suffered a fire in 1962, but were refitted. Marie Dressler, a dress shop, was at No 14. In October 1967, Southampton hosted Ulster Week to promote trade and friendship.

► **SOUTHAMPTON**

The Civic Centre c1955
S151046

People sit admiring this splendid fountain, unfortunately now demolished - a busy road is in its place. Behind is Southampton's Civic Centre housing the civic offices, the police station, Southampton lending library and an art gallery. Its tower is 158 ft high. There is now a fountain by the library entrance, and opposite there are parks. Southampton did not become a city until 1964, after a royal charter was granted.

◄ **SOUTHSEA**
*The Promenade
c1955* S161037

Comic genius Peter Sellers probably came here many times during his childhood. It is seemingly a hot summer's day in Southsea, yet there is just one child wearing shorts. Today everybody would be wearing T-shirts and shorts and slapping on the suntan lotion. Not far from here in Palmerston Road, Handleys of Southsea, a department store and part of the Debenhams group, was 100 years old in 1967.

► **SOUTHSEA**
*Battery Rock
Gardens c1965*
S161122

This was a time when the Beatles and the Rolling Stones could be heard from crackly car radios. The music might have changed, but the scenery hasn't. It is another very hot summer, with sunglasses a common sight, and hundreds gather to worship the sun. Two ladies model the latest conservative fashions, handbags in hand.

SOUTHWICK
High Street c1955 s770005

Southwick is not far from Fareham. Most houses have red front doors, showing that they belong to the local estate; a 19th-century mansion sits on the old priory site. Taken over by the Navy in the Second World War, it was Eisenhower's headquarters in 1944, when he was Supreme Allied Commander. The house, now HMS 'Dryad', still belongs to the Navy, and is the navigation school.

▶ **ST MARY BOURNE**
The School c1955 S635026

This is a lovely environment for children to go to school; here they have been photographed during their break. Situated in School Lane, this primary school is near Andover, and it has approximately 120 pupils aged from 4 to 11 years old. Most of the buildings in St Mary Bourne are built of brick and flint. The church of St Peter stands in the village.

◄ **STOCKBRIDGE**
High Street c1955
S259044

Until 1932, sheep fairs were held here. A Rover 80 is parked to the left of the yellow brick Grosvenor Hotel, the headquarters of the Houghton Club, a fishermen's club controlling fishing on the River Test. This wide street has many handsome buildings. In 1967, one of the Georgian residences with seven bedrooms, two acres and a heated-swimming pool cost £20,000.

◄ *(far left) detail from* S259044

STOKES BAY
The Beach c1955
S717042

Has the sulky-looking girl on the left been told off by her mother? To the right a bikini-clad lady carries a sun umbrella. There are not many bikinis to be spotted here. A typical pram of the day sits on the pebbles. A year later, Britain's finest frogman was to disappear here (see p. 87). Stanley Park is next to the beach. There is a railway station nearby.

STUBBINGTON, *The Parade c1965* S636078

South of Fareham, Stubbington has some attractive areas of modern housing, and the village shopping centre, the Parade, is built around a small green. Stubbington is closely linked with adjacent Crofton. Over the years, as a result of damage sustained during the Second World War, and because of an intensive building programme, the village has undergone a complete transformation.

SWANMORE
The Village Centre
c1965 S424024

There are plenty of people about on this warm sunny day. To the left, children cycle in the road; others sit on benches or the pavement. A cyclist makes his way to Mid Hants Supply Stores in the centre of the village. To the right is a Victorian school and the church of St Barnabas.

SWAY, *The Village c1955* S638012

The man on the left stands still for the photographer. He is dressed in the typical attire of the day; hats and braces were a common sight at this time. Will the cows head straight on or turn right? Opposite the parked car is now a petrol station, and to the right there is a convenience store and post office.

▼ **TADLEY,** *The Parade c1965* T283002

Tadley is not far from the Berkshire border. It looks as if the Austin A30 has hit the post box! The architecture of the Parade is typical of characterless post-war building - but it serves a purpose, for there are a variety of shops for the locals. In the northern part of Tadley stands the church of St Paul. This was completed in 1965, and has a triangular bell tower.

▶ **TOTTON**

The Bypass c1965
T243034

It looks so peaceful ... how times change. North of the bypass are Rumbridge Street and the High Street, offering quieter shopping streets. South of the bypass are late 19th- and 20th-century housing and a large industrial area leading down to Eling creek. Nearby is the brick church of St Winifred, built in 1937.

◀ **TWYFORD**
The Thousand-Year-Old Yew Tree c1955 T284004

Twyford is a large village near Winchester, divided by the main road. This tree can be found in St Mary's churchyard. Behind the yew is Mildmay House; it dates back to about 1700, and was once the rectory. St Mary's Church was designed by Waterhouse, who also designed the Natural History Museum in London.

▶ **UPPER CLATFORD**
The Crook and Shears c1955 U53007

To the right is the Crook and Shears pub, where there is skittles every Thursday night in the Saddle Room. Still independent, it has a range of real ales and guest ales and serves food. Upper Clatford is a mile and a quarter south of Andover. There is a post office and a church here, and the River Anton flows through the valley.

▶ **WALTHAM CHASE**
The Post Office and Stores
c1950 W484006

Waltham Chase originated as a medieval hunting ground not far from Bishop's Waltham. A number of Victorian redbrick houses survive, intermingled with more modern housing. Notice how quiet the road is. Is the lady making her way to the post office? A local contractor, Fred Dyke, owned steam-driven vehicles; lumps of red-hot ash would fall from the fire basket under the boiler onto the road.

◀ **WARSASH**
The Crossroads c1965
W485114

Warsash is situated near Hamble and Park Gate. Straight ahead is the clock tower; this was a water tower supplying Warsash House, which King Edward VII used to visit when he was Prince of Wales. Prior to the Second World War the house was pulled down and replaced with modern houses. An electric clock was installed in 1945. On the right is E G Fox & Son, an estate agent's.

▶ **WATERLOOVILLE**
*London Road
c1965* W486026

Between 1903 and 1935 Waterlooville and Portsmouth were linked by tram. London Road is not the main road to London any more. Here a few Victorian houses survive, mostly rendered, some with verandahs. Further north is a small oak forest. To the north-west is the church of St George, rebuilt in 1970 with a concrete tower. The town is by-passed today, and the M27 is nearby.

◀ **WEEKE**
Stoney Lane c1965
W487009

Weeke lies near Winchester. Plenty of pedestrians walk these footpaths and it is a well-used bus route. Weeke Primary School is down this road - today it has about 280 pupils. Next door is the Adult Continuing Education Centre, a division of Peter Symonds College, attended by the comedian Jack Dee when it was a grammar school. Between 1963 and 1973 John Ashurst was the school's headmaster.

▲ **WEST END,** *Swaythling Road c1950* W428004

If only our roads were still like this. Today, traffic often comes to a standstill here. The shop on the right is no longer a shop, now just a house. Today the pub on the left is the Master Builder, and owned by Wadworth's. Further ahead there is a crossroads: turn left to the Rose Bowl cricket ground and Botley, and go straight ahead for Hamble.

◄ **WEST MEON**
Petersfield Road c1955 W488024

A cyclist, carrying a bag, rides into the distance. The bicycle could be a Hercules Martin made in Birmingham or a Raleigh. A well-finished thatched cottage is accompanied by other slate roofed houses. Nearby is the church of St John Evangelist; in 1963 Guy Burgess, a secret agent for the USSR, who died in Russia, was to be buried in its churchyard.

WEYHILL
The Star Inn and the Post Office c1950
W174014

Weyhill is a roadside settlement of little more than a pub, a post office and the church of St Michael. Weyhill is probably best known for its fairs that sold anything from cattle and horses to cheese and hops; the last cattle fair was held in 1957. The fairground stretched over all the nearby land into the fields beyond. Much of this land is now an industrial estate.

WHITCHURCH, *The White Hart Hotel c1955* W490002

The black and white marks on the kerbstones indicate the junction. This is a small handsome town on the River Test with Georgian buildings that are rendered or red brick. One of the best Georgian buildings is the White Hart Hotel with its rounded corner. To the north-west of the centre is the church of All Hallows, where parish rooms were added in 1974.

WICKHAM
Bridge Street c1950
W491007

Bridge Street curves down to the river. A variety of architecture is to be enjoyed here, from red brick houses to timber-framed cottages. The front doorsteps at the house on the left lead on to the road - not user-friendly, perhaps. In the distance we can see the spire of St Nicholas's Church; inside, the church has no aisles. Behind the photographer is the Square.

WICKHAM, *The Square c1950* W491049

The first shop on the left is the newsagent, and next to it is the Co-op. Today both these shops are as they were, except that the newsagent no longer sells bicycles. The Square remains unchanged but for the removal of the lamp-post and the bus shelter. Behind The Old Tea House (centre right), which is still trading, is a hardware shop. At Christmas there is carol singing in the Square.

111

WINCHESTER
High Street c1955
W107066

Cars can no longer drive through here - it is now pedestrianised. The pavements have been removed and the post box in front of the Butter Cross has moved into Little Minster Street, next to the Vickers shop (right) that is now O$_2$. Next but one to Vickers is an alleyway leading to the Square and Winchester Cathedral. Behind the Butter Cross is Allens. This shop has subsequently been a building society and is now an art shop. On its wall is a sign indicating the Pentice. The first shop on the left is now a Debenhams store selling clothes and beds - the blinds have been removed. Next door is Natwest. Further down on the right is another Debenhams store selling perfume.

WINCHESTER
The Prentice c1955
W107040

Above the second shop on the left, the wood is brown and its walls are cream; the second bay window has been removed. The fifth shop along is Boots, which now occupies three of the shop fronts. On the right the third shop is Clarks.

WOOLSTON, *The Floating Bridge c1960* W468019

Queues wait to board this floating bridge that had run since 1836. In 1977 it was replaced by the Itchen toll bridge. The Vickers Supermarine factory was nearby; here the Spitfire, designed by R J Mitchell, was built. The factory was destroyed by bombing in 1940, and under the new bridge is a memorial to R J Mitchell. Until the 1930s flying boats left here for the Channel Islands.

WOOLSTON, *The Bus Station c1960* W468025

Children impatiently wait with their parents to board the buses. In Southampton, buses took over from trams in the 1940s. Up until 1977 this station was shared with Hants & Dorset motor services. Bristol K5G buses ran into Woolston, and Corporation buses served the floating bridge. Hants & Dorset merged with other companies to form today's First bus company that still runs buses from this station.

YATELEY
The Village c1965
Y6034

The Dog & Partridge sign stands in the middle of the green;
the pub is still trading, and it is the Official Monster Raving Loony
Party's headquarters. Yateley is near the Berkshire border. In 1950,
4,000 people lived here. It became a town in 1975, and now has
28,000 residents. Nearby, St Peter's Church was set fire to in 1979
- the timber porch, built in 1500, survived.

INDEX

Frith Book Co Titles

www.francisfrith.co.uk

The Frith Book Company publishes over 100 new titles each year. A selection of those currently available is listed below. For latest catalogue please contact Frith Book Co.
Town Books 96 pages, approximately 100 photos. **County and Themed Books** 128 pages, approximately 150 photos (unless specified). All titles hardback with laminated case and jacket, except those indicated pb (paperback)

Amersham, Chesham & Rickmansworth (pb)	1-85937-340-2	£9.99	Devon (pb)	1-85937-297-x	£9.99
Andover (pb)	1-85937-292-9	£9.99	Devon Churches (pb)	1-85937-250-3	£9.99
Aylesbury (pb)	1-85937-227-9	£9.99	Dorchester (pb)	1-85937-307-0	£9.99
Barnstaple (pb)	1-85937-300-3	£9.99	Dorset (pb)	1-85937-269-4	£9.99
Basildon Living Memories (pb)	1-85937-515-4	£9.99	Dorset Coast (pb)	1-85937-299-6	£9.99
Bath (pb)	1-85937-419-0	£9.99	Dorset Living Memories (pb)	1-85937-584-7	£9.99
Bedford (pb)	1-85937-205-8	£9.99	Down the Severn (pb)	1-85937-560-x	£9.99
Bedfordshire Living Memories	1-85937-513-8	£14.99	Down The Thames (pb)	1-85937-278-3	£9.99
Belfast (pb)	1-85937-303-8	£9.99	Down the Trent	1-85937-311-9	£14.99
Berkshire (pb)	1-85937-191-4	£9.99	East Anglia (pb)	1-85937-265-1	£9.99
Berkshire Churches	1-85937-170-1	£17.99	East Grinstead (pb)	1-85937-138-8	£9.99
Berkshire Living Memories	1-85937-332-1	£14.99	East London	1-85937-080-2	£14.99
Black Country	1-85937-497-2	£12.99	East Sussex (pb)	1-85937-606-1	£9.99
Blackpool (pb)	1-85937-393-3	£9.99	Eastbourne (pb)	1-85937-399-2	£9.99
Bognor Regis (pb)	1-85937-431-x	£9.99	Edinburgh (pb)	1-85937-193-0	£8.99
Bournemouth (pb)	1-85937-545-6	£9.99	England In The 1880s	1-85937-331-3	£17.99
Bradford (pb)	1-85937-204-x	£9.99	Essex - Second Selection	1-85937-456-5	£14.99
Bridgend (pb)	1-85937-386-0	£7.99	Essex (pb)	1-85937-270-8	£9.99
Bridgwater (pb)	1-85937-305-4	£9.99	Essex Coast	1-85937-342-9	£14.99
Bridport (pb)	1-85937-327-5	£9.99	Essex Living Memories	1-85937-490-5	£14.99
Brighton (pb)	1-85937-192-2	£8.99	Exeter	1-85937-539-1	£9.99
Bristol (pb)	1-85937-264-3	£9.99	Exmoor (pb)	1-85937-608-8	£9.99
British Life A Century Ago (pb)	1-85937-213-9	£9.99	Falmouth (pb)	1-85937-594-x	£9.99
Buckinghamshire (pb)	1-85937-200-7	£9.99	Folkestone (pb)	1-85937-124-8	£9.99
Camberley (pb)	1-85937-222-8	£9.99	Frome (pb)	1-85937-317-8	£9.99
Cambridge (pb)	1-85937-422-0	£9.99	Glamorgan	1-85937-488-3	£14.99
Cambridgeshire (pb)	1-85937-420-4	£9.99	Glasgow (pb)	1-85937-190-6	£9.99
Cambridgeshire Villages	1-85937-523-5	£14.99	Glastonbury (pb)	1-85937-338-0	£7.99
Canals And Waterways (pb)	1-85937-291-0	£9.99	Gloucester (pb)	1-85937-232-5	£9.99
Canterbury Cathedral (pb)	1-85937-179-5	£9.99	Gloucestershire (pb)	1-85937-561-8	£9.99
Cardiff (pb)	1-85937-093-4	£9.99	Great Yarmouth (pb)	1-85937-426-3	£9.99
Carmarthenshire (pb)	1-85937-604-5	£9.99	Greater Manchester (pb)	1-85937-266-x	£9.99
Chelmsford (pb)	1-85937-310-0	£9.99	Guildford (pb)	1-85937-410-7	£9.99
Cheltenham (pb)	1-85937-095-0	£9.99	Hampshire (pb)	1-85937-279-1	£9.99
Cheshire (pb)	1-85937-271-6	£9.99	Harrogate (pb)	1-85937-423-9	£9.99
Chester (pb)	1-85937-382 8	£9.99	Hastings and Bexhill (pb)	1-85937-131-0	£9.99
Chesterfield (pb)	1-85937-378-x	£9.99	Heart of Lancashire (pb)	1-85937-197-3	£9.99
Chichester (pb)	1-85937-228-7	£9.99	Helston (pb)	1-85937-214-7	£9.99
Churches of East Cornwall (pb)	1-85937-249-x	£9.99	Hereford (pb)	1-85937-175-2	£9.99
Churches of Hampshire (pb)	1-85937-207-4	£9.99	Herefordshire (pb)	1-85937-567-7	£9.99
Cinque Ports & Two Ancient Towns	1-85937-492-1	£14.99	Herefordshire Living Memories	1-85937-514-6	£14.99
Colchester (pb)	1-85937-188-4	£8.99	Hertfordshire (pb)	1-85937-247-3	£9.99
Cornwall (pb)	1-85937-229-5	£9.99	Horsham (pb)	1-85937-432-8	£9.99
Cornwall Living Memories	1-85937-248-1	£14.99	Humberside (pb)	1-85937-605-3	£9.99
Cotswolds (pb)	1-85937-230-9	£9.99	Hythe, Romney Marsh, Ashford (pb)	1-85937-256-2	£9.99
Cotswolds Living Memories	1-85937-255-4	£14.99	Ipswich (pb)	1-85937-424-7	£9.99
County Durham (pb)	1-85937-398-4	£9.99	Isle of Man (pb)	1-85937-268-6	£9.99
Croydon Living Memories (pb)	1-85937-162-0	£9.99	Isle of Wight (pb)	1-85937-429-8	£9.99
Cumbria (pb)	1-85937-621-5	£9.99	Isle of Wight Living Memories	1-85937-304-6	£14.99
Derby (pb)	1-85937-367-4	£9.99	Kent (pb)	1-85937-189-2	£9.99
Derbyshire (pb)	1-85937-196-5	£9.99	Kent Living Memories(pb)	1-85937-401-8	£9.99
Derbyshire Living Memories	1-85937-330-5	£14.99	Kings Lynn (pb)	1-85937-334-8	£9.99

Available from your local bookshop or from the publisher

Frith Book Co Titles (continued)

Title	ISBN	Price
Lake District (pb)	1-85937-275-9	£9.99
Lancashire Living Memories	1-85937-335-6	£14.99
Lancaster, Morecambe, Heysham (pb)	1-85937-233-3	£9.99
Leeds (pb)	1-85937-202-3	£9.99
Leicester (pb)	1-85937-381-x	£9.99
Leicestershire & Rutland Living Memories	1-85937-500-6	£12.99
Leicestershire (pb)	1-85937-185-x	£9.99
Lighthouses	1-85937-257-0	£9.99
Lincoln (pb)	1-85937-380-1	£9.99
Lincolnshire (pb)	1-85937-433-6	£9.99
Liverpool and Merseyside (pb)	1-85937-234-1	£9.99
London (pb)	1-85937-183-3	£9.99
London Living Memories	1-85937-454-9	£14.99
Ludlow (pb)	1-85937-176-0	£9.99
Luton (pb)	1-85937-235-x	£9.99
Maidenhead (pb)	1-85937-339-9	£9.99
Maidstone (pb)	1-85937-391-7	£9.99
Manchester (pb)	1-85937-198-1	£9.99
Marlborough (pb)	1-85937-336-4	£9.99
Middlesex	1-85937-158-2	£14.99
Monmouthshire	1-85937-532-4	£14.99
New Forest (pb)	1-85937-390-9	£9.99
Newark (pb)	1-85937-366-6	£9.99
Newport, Wales (pb)	1-85937-258-9	£9.99
Newquay (pb)	1-85937-421-2	£9.99
Norfolk (pb)	1-85937-195-7	£9.99
Norfolk Broads	1-85937-486-7	£14.99
Norfolk Living Memories (pb)	1-85937-402-6	£9.99
North Buckinghamshire	1-85937-626-6	£14.99
North Devon Living Memories	1-85937-261-9	£14.99
North Hertfordshire	1-85937-547-2	£14.99
North London (pb)	1-85937-403-4	£9.99
North Somerset	1-85937-302-x	£14.99
North Wales (pb)	1-85937-298-8	£9.99
North Yorkshire (pb)	1-85937-236-8	£9.99
Northamptonshire Living Memories	1-85937-529-4	£14.99
Northamptonshire	1-85937-150-7	£14.99
Northumberland Tyne & Wear (pb)	1-85937-281-3	£9.99
Northumberland	1-85937-522-7	£14.99
Norwich (pb)	1-85937-194-9	£8.99
Nottingham (pb)	1-85937-324-0	£9.99
Nottinghamshire (pb)	1-85937-187-6	£9.99
Oxford (pb)	1-85937-411-5	£9.99
Oxfordshire (pb)	1-85937-430-1	£9.99
Oxfordshire Living Memories	1-85937-525-1	£14.99
Paignton (pb)	1-85937-374-7	£7.99
Peak District (pb)	1-85937-280-5	£9.99
Pembrokeshire	1-85937-262-7	£14.99
Penzance (pb)	1-85937-595-2	£9.99
Peterborough (pb)	1-85937-219-8	£9.99
Picturesque Harbours	1-85937-208-2	£14.99
Piers	1-85937-237-6	£17.99
Plymouth (pb)	1-85937-389-5	£9.99
Poole & Sandbanks (pb)	1-85937-251-1	£9.99
Preston (pb)	1-85937-212-0	£9.99
Reading (pb)	1-85937-238-4	£9.99
Redhill to Reigate (pb)	1-85937-596-0	£9.99
Ringwood (pb)	1-85937-384-4	£7.99
Romford (pb)	1-85937-319-4	£9.99
Royal Tunbridge Wells (pb)	1-85937-504-9	£9.99
Salisbury (pb)	1-85937-239-2	£9.99
Scarborough (pb)	1-85937-379-8	£9.99
Sevenoaks and Tonbridge (pb)	1-85937-392-5	£9.99
Sheffield & South Yorks (pb)	1-85937-267-8	£9.99
Sherborne (pb)	1-85937-301-1	£9.99
Shrewsbury (pb)	1-85937-325-9	£9.99
Shropshire (pb)	1-85937-326-7	£9.99
Shropshire Living Memories	1-85937-643-6	£14.99
Somerset	1-85937-153-1	£14.99
South Devon Coast	1-85937-107-8	£14.99
South Devon Living Memories (pb)	1-85937-609-6	£9.99
South East London (pb)	1-85937-263-5	£9.99
South Somerset	1-85937-318-6	£14.99
South Wales	1-85937-519-7	£14.99
Southampton (pb)	1-85937-427-1	£9.99
Southend (pb)	1-85937-313-5	£9.99
Southport (pb)	1-85937-425-5	£9.99
St Albans (pb)	1-85937-341-0	£9.99
St Ives (pb)	1-85937-415-8	£9.99
Stafford Living Memories (pb)	1-85937-503-0	£9.99
Staffordshire (pb)	1-85937-308-9	£9.99
Stourbridge (pb)	1-85937-530-8	£9.99
Stratford upon Avon (pb)	1-85937-388-7	£9.99
Suffolk (pb)	1-85937-221-x	£9.99
Suffolk Coast (pb)	1-85937-610-x	£9.99
Surrey (pb)	1-85937-240-6	£9.99
Surrey Living Memories	1-85937-328-3	£14.99
Sussex (pb)	1-85937-184-1	£9.99
Sutton (pb)	1-85937-337-2	£9.99
Swansea (pb)	1-85937-167-1	£9.99
Taunton (pb)	1-85937-314-3	£9.99
Tees Valley & Cleveland (pb)	1-85937-623-1	£9.99
Teignmouth (pb)	1-85937-370-4	£7.99
Thanet (pb)	1-85937-116-7	£9.99
Tiverton (pb)	1-85937-178-7	£9.99
Torbay (pb)	1-85937-597-9	£9.99
Truro (pb)	1-85937-598-7	£9.99
Victorian & Edwardian Dorset	1-85937-254-6	£14.99
Victorian & Edwardian Kent (pb)	1-85937-624-X	£9.99
Victorian & Edwardian Maritime Album (pb)	1-85937-622-3	£9.99
Victorian and Edwardian Sussex (pb)	1-85937-625-8	£9.99
Villages of Devon (pb)	1-85937-293-7	£9.99
Villages of Kent (pb)	1-85937-294-5	£9.99
Villages of Sussex (pb)	1-85937-295-3	£9.99
Warrington (pb)	1-85937-507-3	£9.99
Warwick (pb)	1-85937-518-9	£9.99
Warwickshire (pb)	1-85937-203-1	£9.99
Welsh Castles (pb)	1-85937-322-4	£9.99
West Midlands (pb)	1-85937-289-9	£9.99
West Sussex (pb)	1-85937-607-x	£9.99
West Yorkshire (pb)	1-85937-201-5	£9.99
Weston Super Mare (pb)	1-85937-306-2	£9.99
Weymouth (pb)	1-85937-209-0	£9.99
Wiltshire (pb)	1-85937-277-5	£9.99
Wiltshire Churches (pb)	1-85937-171-x	£9.99
Wiltshire Living Memories (pb)	1-85937-396-8	£9.99
Winchester (pb)	1-85937-428-x	£9.99
Windsor (pb)	1-85937-333-x	£9.99
Wokingham & Bracknell (pb)	1-85937-329-1	£9.99
Woodbridge (pb)	1-85937-498-0	£9.99
Worcester (pb)	1-85937-165-5	£9.99
Worcestershire Living Memories	1-85937-489-1	£14.99
Worcestershire	1-85937-152-3	£14.99
York (pb)	1-85937-199-x	£9.99
Yorkshire (pb)	1-85937-186-8	£9.99
Yorkshire Coastal Memories	1-85937-506-5	£14.99
Yorkshire Dales	1-85937-502-2	£14.99
Yorkshire Living Memories (pb)	1-85937-397-6	£9.99

See Frith books on the internet at www.francisfrith.co.uk

FRITH PRODUCTS & SERVICES

Francis Frith would doubtless be pleased to know that the pioneering publishing venture he started in 1860 still continues today. Over a hundred and forty years later, The Francis Frith Collection continues in the same innovative tradition and is now one of the foremost publishers of vintage photographs in the world. Some of the current activities include:

Interior Decoration

Today Frith's photographs can be seen framed and as giant wall murals in thousands of pubs, restaurants, hotels, banks, retail stores and other public buildings throughout the country. In every case they enhance the unique local atmosphere of the places they depict and provide reminders of gentler days in an increasingly busy and frenetic world.

Product Promotions

Frith products are used by many major companies to promote the sales of their own products or to reinforce their own history and heritage. Frith promotions have been used by Hovis bread, Courage beers, Scots Porage Oats, Colman's mustard, Cadbury's foods, Mellow Birds coffee, Dunhill pipe tobacco, Guinness, and Bulmer's Cider.

Genealogy and Family History

As the interest in family history and roots grows world-wide, more and more people are turning to Frith's photographs of Great Britain for images of the towns, villages and streets where their ancestors lived; and, of course, photographs of the churches and chapels where their ancestors were christened, married and buried are an essential part of every genealogy tree and family album.

Frith Products

All Frith photographs are available Framed or just as Mounted Prints and Posters (size 23 x 16 inches). These may be ordered from the address below. From time to time other products - Address Books, Calendars, Table Mats, etc - are available.

The Internet

Already fifty thousand Frith photographs can be viewed and purchased on the internet through the Frith websites and a myriad of partner sites.

For more detailed information on Frith companies and products, look at these sites:

www.francisfrith.co.uk
www.francisfrith.com
(for North American visitors)

See the complete list of Frith Books at:

www.francisfrith.co.uk

This web site is regularly updated with the latest list of publications from the Frith Book Company. If you wish to buy books relating to another part of the country that your local bookshop does not stock, you may purchase on-line.

For further information, trade, or author enquiries please contact us at the address below:
The Francis Frith Collection, Frith's Barn, Teffont, Salisbury, Wiltshire, England SP3 5QP.
Tel: +44 (0)1722 716 376 Fax: +44 (0)1722 716 881   Email: sales@francisfrith.co.uk

See Frith books on the internet at www.francisfrith.co.uk

FREE PRINT OF YOUR CHOICE

Mounted Print
Overall size 14 x 11 inches (355 x 280mm)

Choose any Frith photograph in this book.
Simply complete the Voucher opposite and return it with your remittance for £2.25 (to cover postage and handling) and we will print the photograph of your choice in SEPIA (size 11 x 8 inches) and supply it in a cream mount with a burgundy rule line (overall size 14 x 11 inches). **Please note: photographs with a reference number starting with a "Z" are not Frith photographs and cannot be supplied under this offer.**
Offer valid for delivery to one UK address only.

PLUS: **Order additional Mounted Prints at HALF PRICE - £7.49 each** (normally £14.99)
If you would like to order more Frith prints from this book, possibly as gifts for friends and family, you can buy them at half price (with no additional postage and handling costs).

PLUS: **Have your Mounted Prints framed**
For an extra £14.95 per print you can have your mounted print(s) framed in an elegant polished wood and gilt moulding, overall size 16 x 13 inches (no additional postage and handling required).

IMPORTANT!

These special prices are only available if you use this form to order . You must use the ORIGINAL VOUCHER on this page (no copies permitted). We can only despatch to one UK address. This offer cannot be combined with any other offer.

Send completed Voucher form to:
The Francis Frith Collection, Frith's Barn, Teffont, Salisbury, Wiltshire SP3 5QP

CHOOSE A PHOTOGRAPH FROM THIS BOOK

Voucher for **FREE** *and Reduced Price Frith Prints*

Please do not photocopy this voucher. Only the original is valid, so please fill it in, cut it out and return it to us with your order.

Picture ref no	Page no	Qty	Mounted @ £7.49	Framed + £14.95	Total Cost £
		1	Free of charge*	£	£
			£7.49	£	£
			£7.49	£	£
			£7.49	£	£
			£7.49	£	£
			£7.49	£	£

Please allow 28 days for delivery. Offer available to one UK address only

* Post & handling		£2.25
Total Order Cost		£

Title of this book . . . .

I enclose a cheque/postal order for £ . . . . made payable to 'The Francis Frith Collection'

OR please debit my Mastercard / Visa / Maestro / Amex card, details below

Card Number

Issue No (Maestro only)   Valid from (Maestro)

Expires   Signature

Name Mr/Mrs/Ms . . . .
Address . . . .
. . . .
. . . .
. . . . Postcode . . . .
Daytime Tel No . . . .
Email . . . .

ISBN: 1-85937-527-8   Valid to 31/12/07

Would you like to find out more about Francis Frith?

We have recently recruited some entertaining speakers who are happy to visit local groups, clubs and societies to give an illustrated talk documenting Frith's travels and photographs. If you are a member of such a group and are interested in hosting a presentation, we would love to hear from you.

Our speakers bring with them a small selection of our local town and county books, together with sample prints. They are happy to take orders. A small proportion of the order value is donated to the group who have hosted the presentation. The talks are therefore an excellent way of fundraising for small groups and societies.

Can you help us with information about any of the Frith photographs in this book?

We are gradually compiling an historical record for each of the photographs in the Frith archive. It is always fascinating to find out the names of the people shown in the pictures, as well as insights into the shops, buildings and other features depicted.

If you recognize anyone in the photographs in this book, or if you have information not already included in the author's caption, do let us know. We would love to hear from you, and will try to publish it in future books or articles.

Our production team

Frith books are produced by a small dedicated team at offices in the converted Grade II listed 18th-century barn at Teffont near Salisbury, illustrated above. Most have worked with the Frith Collection for many years. All have in common one quality: they have a passion for the Frith Collection. The team is constantly expanding, but currently includes:

Paul Baron, Phillip Brennan, Jason Buck, John Buck, Ruth Butler, Heather Crisp, David Davies, Louis du Mont, Isobel Hall, Lucy Hart, Julian Hight, Peter Horne, James Kinnear, Karen Kinnear, Tina Leary, Stuart Login, David Marsh, Lesley-Ann Millard, Sue Molloy, Glenda Morgan, Wayne Morgan, Sarah Roberts, Kate Rotondetto, Dean Scource, Eliza Sackett, Terence Sackett, Sandra Sampson, Adrian Sanders, Sandra Sanger, Julia Skinner, David Smith, Miles Smith, Lewis Taylor, Shelley Tolcher, Lorraine Tuck, Amanita Wainwright and Ricky Williams.

Free Print – see overleaf

Hampshire